FAITH
HOPE &
LOVE

BECKY JANE DICE

MY FAITH

Those of a steadfast mind,
You keep in peace,
Trust in the LORD forever,
God is an everlasting Rock.
With peace of mind,
My faith will not cease,
God is mine forever,
Jesus stands at the door of my soul
    and knocks.

My faith in God is real,
I don't sit around imagining the
worst,
No hand wringing for me,
I don't become stressed out on what
    might be.
Keeping my thoughts on God who
    is real,
He is first,
I see,
The truth sets my soul free.

With God as my constant companion,
He is by my side,
Hand in hand we go,
I let Him be my guide.
When my life on earth is done,
May He open Heaven's gates wide,
Then I will surely know,
I've made it safely to the other side.

🌿🌿🌿🌿🌿🌿🌿🌿🌿🌿🌿🌿🌿🌿🌿🌿🌿

GOD'S LOVE

Love is patient and kind,
God loves me,
Jesus assured me this I know,
His love never ends.
God loves all mankind,
He will take care of you and me,
He says what we reap; we shall sow,
His eternal life is without end.

Love bears all things,
Believes in all things that are good,
Hopes in all things that are grand,
Endures until the end.
God loves the birds that sing,
Neither reap nor gather food,
God takes care of them isn't it grand,
His love is without end.

With love so pure and constant,
As I am, right here, right now,
God loves even me,
He loves me when I am at my best.
When I am angry and rant,
He loves me and I can't imagine how.
But I abide in Him, He with me,
I give Him my best.

GOD'S PROSPERITY

God's abundance is mine to use,
To enjoy,
To share,
An abundance without end.
I see it when each day is new,
It is mine to enjoy,
God is there,
He is my constant friend.

God is able to provide,
He knows my needs,
When I have too much,
He knows when I lack.
He shelters me when I want to hide,
He knows my good deeds,
Helps me when I am in a clutch,
He gives but doesn't take it back.

God has no limits of what He gives to me,
I give thanks in the morn,
Reflecting on my blessings,
Overflowing without measure.
His love is free,
It was given to me before I was born.
God is the Supreme Being,
In whom I treasure.

GOD'S GUIDANCE

You are my Rock,
My fortress when I want to hide,
When I am lost,
Guiding me when I wander.
God's gentle love is my Rock.
Filling me with peace from on High,
He loves me when I was lost,
Giving me answers as I ponder.

In a quiet moment of reflection,
I return to the center of my soul,
With God's gentle love as my guide,
I know I have hope for this day.
In the quiet day of reflection,
He inspires my soul,
I let Him be the guide,
My heart will not sway.

His guidance is crucial,
It enlighten my mind,
Inspires my soul,
I let God's wisdom help me chose a path.
He brings my heart instant renewal,
God is kind,
Loving me, this I know,
Setting me on the right path.

A SPIRIT OF HARMONY

I release judgment as I respond,
A spirit of harmony,
A spirit of love,
If my success in relationship harms another.
I have a spiritual bond,
Between God and me,
One spirit of love,
Loving one another.

In the midst of disagreement,
A judgment of criticism.
If I hurt another in word,
Or in deed,
I ask for forgiveness of time spent.
Also hurting Him,
In the stillness His voice is heard,
His forgiveness is all I need.

A spirit of harmony,
Sets my heart free,
I connect with the love of God within,
My soul finds serenity.
A heart full of love,
A spirit of harmony,
Is all that I need,
I am of one accord.

PRAYER

Prayer by prayer,
Day by Day,
I build a life of prayer,
Looking to Jesus as my example.
A life of prayer,
Points me to Jesus each day,
I know He is there,
My heart is full.

Prayer brings healing power,
Jesus prayed for all the people,
He could touch that one close by,
Or at a distance of many miles.
He healed them that very hour,
Jesus loved the people,
Comforting them when they cry,
Turning frowns into smiles.

Prayer by prayer,
What I faithfully believe in,
I draw to me as a magnet attracting good,
Prayer builds the cornerstones.
My daily communion with God
starts with prayer,
I hear His voice in the wind,
His Scriptures are as nourishing food,
He whispers, "You're never alone."

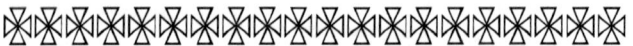

PREPARED

God has prepared His Kingdom,
In my heart,
Where it will stay,
Sustaining me.
His great Kingdom,
Will quiet my heart,
Help me this day,
Nourishing me.

God prepared me for life,
My mind learns from others,
His spirit gives me power,
I know right from wrong.
What I choose in this life,
Whether I help others,
How I view a flower,
Keeps me strong.

When I stand before God,
I am on His right hand,
I hope Jesus will say,
"Come, you are blessed by my Father.
My Father God,
You take a stand,
And do not sway,
You stood by the Father.

Inherit the Kingdom,
Prepared for you,
Free in Spirit,
Be renewed of heart.
Enter into My Kingdom,
Chosen for you,
Each prayer you sent I heard it,
You prayed from your heart.

OUT OF THE DARKNESS

Out of the darkness,
My LORD drew me,
He created in me a clean heart,
Putting a right spirit within.
His love is as a sweet caress,
Giving me serenity,
Restoring in me a new heart,
I can say, "Amen!"

Out of the darkness I now see,
God's glory and love,
He has shown me the Savior,
My Master; my King.
I plea on bent knee,
I see His great light from above,
I answer His knock upon my heart's door,
It is through His grace I can sing.

His saving grace has pulled me,
Out of the darkness that was in my heart,
Cleansing my soul,
I praise His holy name.
This is why He created me,
Opening the eyes of my heart,
And I know,
Because into His truth I came.

Each day I pray to my LORD,
Keep this darkness away,
I want to see only You,
Who revived my heart again.
Shining in the light of Your glory LORD,
Giving me this today,
A heart that is new,
Praise Jesus' holy name.

GOD WITH ME

There has been times when in my life,
A situation that seems odd,
I didn't understand it,
And released the outcome to divine wisdom.
When I need answers about life,
I learn to let go, and let God,
He knows about it,
As questions come.

When I discover that my courage is lacking,
I go to God because He cares,
Giving me wisdom to stand firm,
He goes with me.
This I can sing,
He is the Father of the King,
He answers prayer,
God is with me, this I affirm.

God is with me; I give my problems to Him,
I give Him what challenges I have,
My tears,
My pain,
I give it all to Him.
His love is as a sweet salve,
Soothing my fears,
I praise Jesus' holy name.

I stop trying to be in control,
Affirming God can do a better job,
He does more than I could hope for,
Blessing me more than I deserve.
Yes, He comforts my soul,
When I let go, and let God,
He is with me forevermore,
It is He I serve.

PASS IT ON

Love one another,
Is God's great command.
I share God's love with everyone,
Through kind words and deeds,
Each one is my sister and brother,
Each woman and man,
As I pass on a kindness to that one,
I plant a good seed.

God says love one another, pass it on,
A never-ending journey,
A world of the love of God in expression,
Blessing my family and friends,
Love is free to each one,
Let it start first in me,
God loves you; pass it on,
A true love without end.

I AM BLESSED

I am blessed beyond measure,
God's goodness fills me,
I am fully satisfied,
Filled by the light of His love.
When I think about it, Oh the treasure,
That God could love even me,
For me Jesus was crucified,
Preparing a place in Heaven above.

I am blessed with spiritual prosperity,
I have all I need.
When I put God first,
He blesses me greatly,
Oh sweet serenity.
Upon His word I feed,
Quenching my thirst,
What a blessing to me.

The Spirit Divine is the source of all
goodness,
It enriches my life,
Each need is met,
Whether it be health of wisdom,
God knows best,
He blesses my life,
Jesus' death paid the debt,
His resurrection assured a place in
His Kingdom.

SPIRIT OF GOD

The Spirit of God made me,
His breath gave me life,
God is within me this very hour,
I give Him thanks for renewal of my heart.
The Spirit of God helped me,
Past the mundane things of life,
The beauty of a springtime flower,
The sweet singing of a lark.

He has shown me even a rain shower,
Nourishes the plants above and below,
Even the changes of each season,
Is will by God's Spirit.
All is His even the minutes and hours,
The owl and the crow,
Even that beyond reason,
All He has to do is whisper and I hear it.

The life of God is active within,
Yes, willed by His spirit,
He gives me strength and courage,
He is always active and ongoing.
When He renews my heart again,
I am moved by His Spirit,
He is wiser than a sage,
God is all knowing.

SPIRIT OF TRUTH

When the Spirit of
truth comes,
he will guide you
into all truth
He will not speak
on His own
God is constant
and true
shining the light of
revelation of good
awaiting my acceptance
of Him.

Living in the moment
of awareness of God
I am always
and forever
being guided to
what is highest good
moments in which
a challenge seems unsolvable
unattainable
a solution becomes clear
when the Spirit of truth
comes
He will guide me
into all truth.

FOCUS ON GOD

If a rain shower should delay my plans,
I just remember God's divine order of things,
For He directs my path,
His light shines my way.
He tells me rain is good for the land,
It nourishes the plants and bugs with wings,
The bright flowers in my path,
I thank God for the rain each day.

The changing of the seasons,
Tell me God is active always,
His creation ongoing,
I keep my thoughts positive.
He does things for a reason,
He will be with me all of my days,
I don't give into moaning,
Like everything in creation, I am His.

GOD IS EVERYWHERE

God is everywhere present,
Keeping me safe,
Keeping me secure at all times,
If I become frightened in the night.
I remember His Son He sent,
God's love keeps me safe,
My fears are tamed,
He is with me until morning's light.

God is everywhere and I am calm,
In stormy situations of life,
I remember He will never leave me,
Nor forsake me ever.
God is shining in the midst and I am calm,
I give to Him my anxiety and strife,
He calms my fears tossed on stormy seas,
God is so clever.

God is everywhere so I do not fear,
Calling upon God transforms confusion into peace,
The God of light is shining through me,
Around me.
In each situation I feel God is near,
The calm that He brings will never cease,
I go to God on bent knee,
And I feel God everywhere around me.

GOD'S GRACE

God's grace revives me,
Sustaining me constantly,
Renewing my spirit,
Giving me breath each day,
God's grace surrounds me,
Loves me,
When He whispers I hear it,
He gives me courage to face the day.

God's grace fills me with new energy,
Stimulation to think positive thoughts,
His grace continually surrounds me,
Loves me,
Sustains me,
I'm happy with all the things I've got.
From His fullness He fills me,
He always watches me.

God's grace honors me,
I am a child of God,
Who loves me unconditionally,
Knowing this, I understand truly.
My flaws I now see,
Are in the hands of God,
They are opportunities,
For Him to work through me.

FORGIVENESS

Bear with one another,
Forgive any misdeed,
In an atmosphere of forgiveness,
Relationships flourish.
If anyone has a complaint against another,
Forgiveness is what you need,
In a spirit of forgiveness,
Love within your heart will nourish.

The act of forgiveness,
Is a starting-over point for you,
It springs forth from the Spirit of God,
Within me.
For the act of forgiveness,
Will renew,
Your relationship with God,
And you and me.

Just as the LORD has forgiven me,
I must also forgive the offender,
Bear with one another,
Love that one.
Overlook the flaws you see,
Forgive often,
And love one another,
Until life here on earth is done.

ALL THINGS NEW

If anyone is in Christ,
There is a new creation,
Everything old has passed away,
We are always learning.
Always moving forward looking to Christ,
Our learning is never done,
We find inner strength when we pray,
A new song we can sing.

Growing spiritually we notice blessings,
That change brings,
Everything has become new,
We move ahead.
We worship God in the songs we sing,
We soar high as if on angel's wings,
No need to feel blue,
Put on a smile instead.

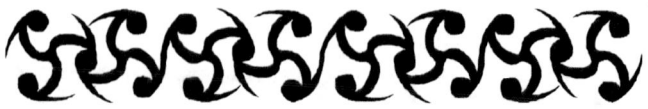

WORDS

Whatever my God say's that I will speak,
My words are natural,
Joyful expressions of the love of God,
Within me.
Words are powerful for those who speak,
They are never dull,
They come from God,
This I see.

Words are for healing,
God moves through words,
Helping to encourage,
And inspire.
Words are wonderful things,
Wonderful words,
They quiet the inner rage,
They quench the fire.

An expression of God's love,
His kindness within,
I always seem to know just what to say.
I know God is there,
The right words of love,
That comes from within,
Each time I pray,
Words I love to share.

TRUSTING

Happy are those who trust in the LORD,
God assures them prosperity.
God loves me,
When I realize my worth,
I know I'm a creation of my LORD.
My eyes are opened and I see,
A need to share what He has done
for me.
With all on Earth.

God gives me confidence,
To pursue my heart's desire,
I am fulfilled.
My journey to reach these goals,
Or the confidence,
When He sets my path afire.
I am in the center of His will,
God loves me, this I know.

HEALING

Bless the LORD, Oh my soul,
And all that is within me,
God who satisfies,
Goodness that inspires,
Let me always grow,
Let my eyes always see,
May the truth never ever die,
Or quench the fire.

May my youth be renewed like the eagle's,
God's spirit within me,
Holds the promise of new life,
I am healed.
My spirit soars as the eagle,
I feel His life within me,
In the midst of strife,
I am healed.

God's spirit is within me,
Yes, I am made strong,
Bless the LORD, Oh my soul,
I am happy and free.
Inspiration comes to me,
And I sing all day long.
Jesus loves me this I know,
Because He promised me.

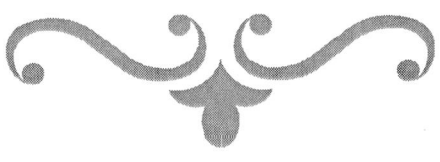

IN THE MOMENT

I am living in the moment,
Aware of more than my reasoning tells me,
In every moment God directs me,
Enriching my life in many ways.
God is with me every moment,
His energy enlivens and heals me,
His wisdom guides me,
Each and every day.

I am enfolded in His presence,
Lingering in the moment,
In prayer and meditation,
All feelings of tension fade away,
I am thankful for the peace He sent,
That very hour, that very moment.
In meditation,
Satan cannot sway.

My concerns fade into nothingness,
I am enfolded in God's loving arms,
Living for Him,
To fear I have no reason.
I know I am blessed,
Because God keeps away harm,
And draws me to Him,
I abide in Him for a season.

FREEDOM

The LORD sets everyone free,
He opens the eyes of the blind,
And lifts up those who are bowed down.
The LORD loves the righteous,
Bless my soul and all this is within me,
The Creator of all mankind,
Can put a smile where once was a frown,
He has done it for us.

If anyone is in Christ,
There is a new creation,
Everything old has passed away,
Everything has become new.
Those who trust in the LORD,
Will create a great nation,
If they pray night and day,
This they must do.

Whatever they ask for in prayer,
With faith they will receive,
The LORD will set them free,
He will open their eyes,
Lift them up when they bow down
in prayer.
He won't let Satan deceive,
When they go down on their knees,
He will hear their cries.

LIFT UP YOUR HANDS

Lift up yours hands to the holy place,
And bless the LORD,
May He, the maker of heaven and earth,
Bless you from Zion.
Let us seek His face,
Blessed is the name of the LORD,
May He give us a blessing not a curse,
May we be meek, not like a lion.

Hosanna to the Son of David,
Yes, Hosanna to the highest in Heaven!
Lift up your face,
To the maker of heaven and earth,
Jesus has risen from the dead.
Lift up your hands toward heaven,
You are God's holy race,
You He will not curse.

He will feed His flock like a Shepherd,
And will gather the lambs into His arms.
Let all who take refuge in His name,
Hide with His protection over them,
Even when we whisper we are heard.
There is safety in His arms,
Power in His name,
Lift your hands up to Him.

DIVINE LIFE

God saw everything that He made,
And indeed it was good.
There was evening,
And there was morning.
Creation's foundation was laid,
Everything fit, as it should,
And the angels sing,
It was a glorious thing.

As it is in springtime,
Flowers once again bloom,
Gardens and field team with life,
A cycle of new life and growth continues,

Just as the Earth is renewed in the springtime.
I am renewed as that new flower that blooms,
I have a new life,
Everything is new.

I sense oneness each and every day,
When I connect with God,
In prayer and meditation,
I recognize the perfection within me.
I give expression to it each day,
With faith in God,
Hope and wisdom,
I am strengthened by the divine life
within me.

PEACE OF MIND

The LORD is my shepherd,
I shall not want,
He leads me beside still waters,
He restores my soul.
When I call on Him my voice is heard,
When I am hungry and gaunt,
My problems they are Yours,
You love me, this I know.

The LORD is my peace of mind,
He answers my prayers,
Like a river my life flows,
Gently in absolute serenity.
The LORD is with me all the time,
I know He cares,
When I abide in Him I grow,
He is my eyes when I cannot see.

The LORD is with me always,
He gives me wisdom,
And answers to my most puzzling questions,
Gives me a smile, instead of a frown,
The LORD is with me all of my days,
And a place in His heavenly Kingdom,
When life here on earth is done,
I have no cause to be down.

HE RESTORES MY SOUL

He restores my soul,
He is the joy of my salvation,
I am one with my Creator,
Uplifting, fulfilling.
When in need to Him I go,
In the morning or when the day is done,
I go to the Creator.
I feel He is willing.

He restores my soul,
When I am not able to get away,
My problems are before me,
And are bigger than life.
I pray and He quiets my soul,
The Spirit speaks when I don't know
what to say.
He gives me peace and serenity,
And I am able to face life.

He restores my soul,
And gives me a sweet retreat,
I get away and go before the throne,
And I know I am not alone.
I shut the door and open my soul,
The Scriptures are as sweet meat,
When I am shown,
He restores my soul.

SEEK THE LORD

Seek the LORD and His strength,
Seek His presence continually,
Live with an enthusiasm,
And expect the blessings of life.
Believe in Him, He is your strength,
Seek the LORD on bent knee,
Worship the LORD in hymn,
Seek Him for the answers in your life.

Seek the LORD for inner peace,
Live in harmony,
Always loving one another,
Forever abiding in Him.
Pray and do not cease,
And He will help you to see,
Honor your father and mother,
Go to God even when you cannot see Him.

Seek the LORD and do not worry,
Do not let fear hold you back,
Instead go to Him in prayer,
Expect a blessing each day of your life,
Be at peace; do not hurry,
Be always filled don't lack,
Go to the throne for He is always there,
Seek Him each day of your life.

OH, MY STRENGTH

Oh, my strength,
I will sing praises unto the LORD,
He is my fortress,
In times of trouble.
He is my strength,
I delight on His every word,
He helps me in my distress,
My blessings double.

He is my strength when I lack,
My courage when I sigh,
My courage when I fear
He gives me sunshine,
When my mood is black,
He gives me happiness when I cry,
I sense when He is near,
And I am find.

The LORD is my fortress,
The solid rock in which I stand,
Gentle as a river,
And hard as a Father disciplining
his child.
Be my strength, my fortress,
Help me go on when I don't think
I can,
Be my warmth when I shiver,
And help this heart so wild.

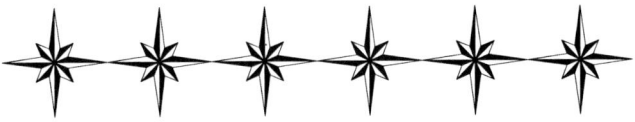

LORD, HEAR ME

Oh LORD, hear me as I pray,
Listen to my cry,
You hear my voice in the morning,
You hear it at night.
I go to You each day,
You hear my every sigh,
You hear me when I sing,
You are interested in my plight.

Oh LORD, hear me when I call,
I bring You my requests,
And wait expectantly,
Please, listen to me.
Lift me up when I fall,
I give You my best,
When I cannot see,
Help me; this is my plea.

When I come to You in the morn,
Please, take my hand,
Be my guide,
Let me hide in You.
You were there the day I was born,
You help me when I don't think I
can,
Dry my tears when I cry,
Oh LORD, hear me when I pray to You.

LET US SING

Let us sing,
With joy unto the LORD,
We must praise Him,
Bring honor to His name,
We make a joyful noise when we sing,
Singing glory to the LORD,
To the joy only He can give,
This should be our greatest aim.

Without His love I could not sing,
My strength would evaporate like water,
In the summer heat.
No more to return,
Filled with unconfessed sin,
I must go to the Father,
When I sing the words are sweet,
And they help me learn.

The LORD loves whatever is just and good,
And His unfailing love fills the earth,
He spoke and heaven and earth were created,
He breathed the word and the stars were born.
The LORD did it because He could.
He brings us good and not a curse,
For me He patiently waited.

When we sing to the LORD,
He stands firm,
He looks down from Heaven above,
And smiles when He hears our voices.
Let us sing to the LORD,
This we can affirm,
He is the God of love,
When we make the right choices.

Let us sing for His glory,
Because He knows our hearts,
And understands everything we do,
So let us sing all day long.
We know the story,
He was there from the start,
He was there when the earth was new,
This should be our song.

GOD, MY REFUGE

I find rest in the shadow of the Almighty,
He alone is my refuge,
My place of safety,
He is my God,
For He rescues me,
He is my refuge,

When sin tempts me,
I trust in God.

He shields me with His promises,
An armor of protection.
I do not fear the terrors of the night,
Nor fear the dangers of the day.
The LORD tells me I am His,
He is second to none,
In the darkness He is my light,
An answer to my prayer.

I do not dread the plague that stalks
in darkness,
Nor disaster that strikes at mid-day,
Even if a thousand fall by my side,
And many die around me,
His protection is as a sweet caress.
When I stop to pray,
His arms open wide,
And they enfold around me.

If I make the LORD my refuge,
If I make the Most High my shelter,
No evil can touch me,
No plague will assail.
God will send His angels,
And evil will scatter helter skelter.
Satan's temptations won't lure me,
I will not fail.

God's angels protect me where ever I go,
Stop me before I strike my foot against a stone.
I will trample down lions,
Crush poisonous serpents beneath my feet,
He will raise me up when I am low,
Comfort me when I a moan,
My fears, they are gone,
God's protection, oh now sweet.

CREATION OF LIGHT

I am God's creation of light,
A whole being of spirit, mind and body,
Light has no part of darkness,
When there is light you know God is there.
His way is right,
This He told to me,
His love is as a sweet caress,
He lets me know He cares.

My spirit gives me connection with God,
I understand He is eternal life,
It radiates within me,
And from me to renew.
My mind fathoms the existence of God,
He is a witness in my life,
God's light shines in me,
My spirit is renewed.

All anxiety and confusion take flight,
I acknowledge god's wisdom,
A light in my soul,
God is everywhere,
This I affirm, I am God's creation of light,
Destined for His heavenly Kingdom,
I am blessed of soul,
Because God will be there.

AWARENESS OF GOD

The awareness of God,
Runs through me,
Around me in a great light,
It fills me with the gladness of His presence,
I am aware of God,
When He whispers to me,
"Trust me when nothing seems right,
When nothing makes sense."

When I am aware of God by my side,
I quietly slip my hand into His.
He is much more than me,
And I am His child.
He comforts me when I cry,
Tells me I am His,
And helps me see,
He tamed my heart when it was wild.

In the awareness of God time is no more,
I learn His ways,
I know a better way to live,
I am blessed and my cup overflows.
When Jesus knocks at the door,
He tells me, "I am the Way."
I have something better to give,
When I am in the awareness of God my
heart knows.

THANK YOU

I give thanks for my heart,
Because God is there,
His my strength and my might,
I am His creation.
He knew me from the start,
I know He cares,
God blessed my heart and made it right,
I am a child of God, His creation.

I give thanks for God's healing power,
I say thank you again and again,
To the God of strength and my courage,
He renews my heart each day,
Yes, every hour.
He forgave me of my sin,
Freed me from a filthy cage,
That housed my heart day after day.

I saw thank you,
For creating in me a new heart, Oh LORD.
Open the eyes of my heart,
Help me shine in the light of Your glory.
Yes, Oh LORD, I do thank You,
You are my one and only LORD,
I lift up to You my heart,
Hand in hand we walk, You and me.

EXPERIENCE THE JOY

What an uplifting
fulfilling
He restores my soul
My heart is renewed
turning to God
within
I experience the joy.

I am one with
my Creator
a spiritual retreat
I turn within
to that quiet of my soul
and I experience His joy.

Here I am alone
with God
no words are necessary
full in the moment
knowing I am His
I am restored
by a power
greater than I.
In the presence of God,
I know that I am
one with my Creator
and I experience the joy.

WHEN YOU SAID SEARCH FOR ME

"When you search for Me," says God,
"You will find me always.
If you seek me with all your heart,
I will let you find Me."
Whenever I want to feel closer to God,
I close the world out and pray,
I plea don't let Your spirit depart,
Take my heart and renew me.

Whenever I go in search of God,
I find Him,
He is closer than a brother,
He is my gentle and loving Heavenly
Father.
When I seek after God,
It is no whim,
He is my God, there is no other,
My Heavenly Father.

I don't have to imaging what God
looks like,
I only need to look around me,

GOD'S COMFORT

When I seem caught up in confusion
and woe,
When everything seems wrong,
Or I share in fear,
I go to God and He eases my pain,
I always find this so.
He kept me strong,
Takes away my tears,
And keeps me sane.

When I know my loved ones are
safe,
My friends to,
When I know they are enjoying life,
I can rest assured in my LORD,
For when they are safe,
My faith in God is renewed,
For I know in this life,
They are right with the LORD.

God cares about me and then I'm sure,
I remember my loved one,
And keep them in my prayer,
Every morning and night.
"God, I pray that my loved ones who are unsure,
Of making it into Your Heavenly Kingdom.
If they are lonely, show them You care,
If sin hides you from their sight.

If they are afraid and cry,
May they feel Your loving presence,
This very hour,
This very day.
May Your name be on theirs lips when
they sigh,
Help them make sense,
When life goes sour,
In Jesus name I pray.

SPIRITUAL POWER

I am an expression
of the loving power
of my LORD
my God
Jesus the ultimate
example of spiritual
power for gave
His persecutors
His example is priceless
His example so true
a lesson for me
and you.

As we invites God's
forgiveness into our hearts
were transformed
and in one accord
our bad thoughts replaced
no anger is there
thoughts of love abound
an expression of God's
loving power.

SPIRITUAL BRIDGES

Dear LORD Your Spirit in me dwells,
Increase my awareness of You.
You help me cross the bridges before me,
Overcoming obstacles in my way.
I know without a debt I can tell,
All my troubles You knew,
Before I could even see,
Before I could pray.

You are much bigger than any problem could be,
And You build a spiritual bridge so I can cross over.
You are bigger than the Evil One,
Who throws temptation in my way.
Build that spiritual bridge before me,
Let me safely cross over,
Squash the Evil One,
Under Your thumb when I pray.

God, Your Spirit is within,
And all around me,
Guide me over the bridges before me,
I am Your child, Oh LORD,
Conquer sin,
Banish the temptations that assail me,
Battle the Evil One for me,
And forever be my LORD.

GOD'S LOVE

God's love is His sword but it does
not cut,
And His love is unending,
It will remain even after life on the earth
ends,
And flows from mountain top to
mountain top.
Is gives feely and cannot be bought,
How precious, His love is unending.
We think tomorrow and the promise He
Sends,
They come and won't stop.

God's love is as a field of wildflowers,
Although as the wildflowers, it does not
wither and die.
I take delight in the fact that it is from the
heart,
When my tears fall like showers,
And I can only sigh,
I know His love won't depart,
And my heart will sing.

God's love draws us nigh,
He is a fortress in times of trouble,
And we find shelter in Him above.
For when we are old,
And our hearts sigh,
Through this life we stumble,
We will find truth and love,
And our hearts will never grow old.

ANGELS

Look around you; take heart,
You may not see them but angels are there,
Right beside you,
And all around you.
When in the night you wake with a start,
Or you fall into a sinful snare,
Your guardian angel is beside you,
And keeps you safe until the day is new.
Don't waver over a bad choice,
Or fret when you are alone,
Because angels will minister unto you,
Or when you face a bully let not your heart
take flight,
The LORD has given the angel a voice,
This angel is of God's own,
So don't fear angels will protect you,
They stand firm for what is right.

Whatever the situation, you're not alone,
Because angels are near.
Who are these angels around us?
They are ministering spirits;
God sends them from above,
They are there when you dash your toe
against a stone,
So you have nothing to fear,
Because angels are all around us,
They have a voice and our hearts heart it.

I THANKED THE LORD

I thanked the LORD today,
For His tender mercies,
And for His Word so true.
And His Son's gift or eternal life.
I thanked the LORD, who doesn't sway,
Like a storm tossed sea,
When the morning is new,
And I struggle with pain and strife.

I thanked the LORD for they grand tomorrow,
When we will all live,
With no hatred, no more fears,
No more fussing or fighting each other.
I thanked the LORD for taking away my sorrow.
And a sweet life to live,
Where there is no more pain or tears,
Just a time when we'll love each other.

A GREAT DAY

I will be a great day when everyone will
love one another,
And quit hating their fellow man,
God said love one and all,
No matter what.
It will be a great day when no war threatens
to smother,
And God's people will take a stand,

Hatred will take a fall,
And harsh words don't rip and out.

It will be a great day when there will be no
more pain,
No more tears,
No sorrow,
Just harmony and love.

A great day when there won't be sin that
stains,
Or fears,
Just a promise of a grand tomorrow,
In Christ's Kingdom above.